Greatest Landscapes

STUNNING PHOTOGRAPHS THAT INSPIRE AND ASTONISH

Foreword by GEORGE STEINMETZ

Text by SUSAN TYLER HITCHCOCK

NATIONAL GEOGRAPHIC
WASHINGTON, D.C.

CONTENTS

PAGE 1: GIANT'S PLAYGROUND, NAMIBIA | Quiver trees, a species of aloe, reach toward the desert night sky. | *Uge Fuertes Sanz*

PAGES 2–3: AMBOSELI NATIONAL PARK, KENYA | Elephants follow well-worn footpaths to graze on the vibrant grasses of Lake Amboseli. | *George Steinmetz*

OPPOSITE: MOUNT RAINIER, WASHINGTON | Sunrise brings pastel tones to Reflection Lakes. | *Marc Adamus*

PAGES 6–7: YELLOWSTONE NATIONAL PARK, WYOMING | Microorganisms color the superheated waters of Grand Prismatic Spring. | *George Steinmetz*

PAGES 8–9: ROCK ISLANDS, PALAU | A boat's wake streaks white across the archipelago's waters. | *Ian Shive*

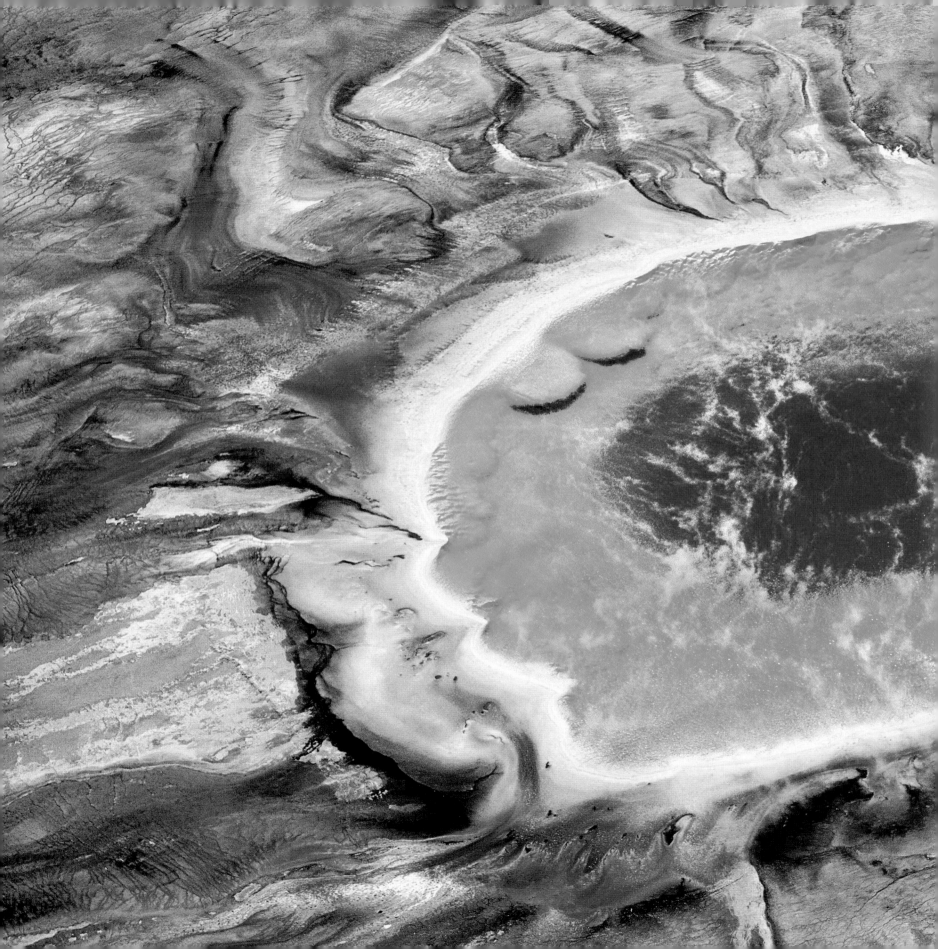

When I was a young man, I decided to leave the comforts of the world I

knew in Southern California. I bought a one-way ticket to Europe and went on a long hitch-hiking trip across Africa. My mother forbade me to go, and the only money I had was from a summer job.

I didn't know much about Africa, but it was the most foreign place I could imagine: the antithesis of suburbia. I didn't know much about photography either but figured I should bring a camera so I could take pictures of strange places filled with animals and native people in exotic garb, like the ones I had seen while leafing through the pages of *National Geographic*.

I bought a high-tech backpack and filled it with stuff I thought I might need: Italian hiking shoes, a camera and a lot of film, a stove that ran on all kinds of fuel—even a snakebite kit. Then I set out to discover the world as a solitary traveler. I really didn't know what I was doing, but I had a burning curiosity to see what was over the horizon—and to try my luck as a photographer.

Mostly I took a lot of bad pictures, but I also got a few good ones and eventually learned from my mistakes. It was there that I started to dream of becoming a National Geographic photographer, and I stuck with it. And now, having worked for *National Geographic* magazine for 30 years, I feel lucky that my dream came true.

PAGES 10–11: GREEN BLUFF, WASHINGTON | Brilliant red autumn leaves enliven a quiet country lane. | *Chip Phillips*

PAGES 12–13: SVALBARD, NORWAY | Small black-and-white dovekies *(Alle alle)* dot the gray sky as they return to their nests. | *Paul Nicklen*

PAGES 14–15: CAPE TOWN, SOUTH AFRICA | A long camera exposure captures evening fog rolling across Kloof Nek and Signal Hill. | *Eric Nathan*

OPPOSITE: LENÇÓIS MARANHENSES NATIONAL PARK, BRAZIL | The rainy season fills pockets between barchan dunes along Brazil's northeastern coast. | *George Steinmetz*

In those early years it seemed like I was always the young punk on every trip. Well, now I find that I'm often the oldest punk on the trip—but the spirit of my adventures is exactly the same.

Sometimes people ask me to share a favorite picture that I've shot. The answer to that one is simple: It's always "the next one." What's important is not just getting the picture; it's *wanting* to get the next picture. It's the wanting that propels you forward.

While I may be known for the landscapes that I've photographed, I see myself more as a journalist and a storyteller. When I arrive in a place, I try to respond to what I see and tell the story of the land. There are no rules or guidelines in that pursuit—except to follow your curiosity and instinct, and try to learn from your mistakes.

With a static subject like a landscape, it might seem strange to try to capture a precise moment. But sometimes the trick is just that: the time when a boat jets through a turquoise passageway between tropical islands, or birds take flight over a glassy lake at dawn. Just as often, though, that magical moment is the stillness of a place, when *nothing* is happening. It's then that you see the sun draw bright green out of a lake, or the pattern of the land, like the web of elephant grazing paths as seen from above on pages 2–3.

There is an old saying that bad weather is a photographer's best friend. But the reality is that every situation is an opportunity, and the challenge is to figure out how to make the best of it. Great landscape photography is like jazz—yet another form of improv—where intuition and spontaneity intersect. I hope you will experience those wondrous collisions in the inspired pages that follow.

—George Steinmetz

OPPOSITE: SAHARA, CHAD | Sandstone pinnacles rise from orange dunes of the Karnasai Valley. | *George Steinmetz*

O, Wind, if Winter comes, can *Spring* be

SPR

far behind? ~ Percy Bysshe Shelley

Something stirs deep within.

Things start to move. Solid ice softens and tends toward a trickle. A warmer sun strikes the desert, the hillsides, the mountaintops. Buds bulge; fronds unfurl. Gauzy colors, pink and chartreuse, whisper through the landscape, as sweet and subtle as a watercolor wash. Spring starts quietly, but here it comes. Time to rise and shine. No wonder the Greeks embodied this moment in a lovely young maiden, emerging annually from Hades' darkness.

The ancients drew the calendar by the seasons. For them, the spring equinox was the day the year began. It is that moment of balance between daylight and darkness, the moment from which the light grows. Sunrise comes earlier every morning. Daylight spills into the evening, ever later every night.

And now the flowers. Pale purple crocuses poke through old snow. Sunny narcissuses stand and nod. Peach trees blush into bloom, pleasing the senses as gloriously as the fruit their flowers foretell. Light, color, fragrance fill the air.

Once the landscape has a sure foothold on the season, all the world comes alive. Tree leaves stretch out to full size and flutter, catching the sunlight that is their food. Spring greens pop up everywhere. Verdant fields increase in abundance. All too soon mowing time will be here.

April is the cruelest month, the poet T. S. Eliot told us, and in the weeks before it's impossible to know why. Surely spring embodies the greatest affirmation of life: new birth in every direction. All seems, for a fleeting moment, to affirm the everlasting. Yet with all that beauty come first losses too. Colors fade. Flowers wilt and shrivel. Blossoms spent, each delicate beginning makes way for summer industry. The first bloom of spring becomes a memory impossible to hold steady as we travel into the rest of the year.

ISLE OF SKYE, SCOTLAND | Verdant grasses swathe the land around the tower of rock known as Castle Ewen. | *Kerstin Enderlein*

TUSCANY, ITALY | A single bale of hay sits in a golden field. | *Frank Krahmer*

OPPOSITE: **ARU ISLANDS, INDONESIA** | An adult male greater bird-of-paradise greets the day on Wokam Island. | *Tim Laman*

PREVIOUS PAGES: **CORNWALL, ENGLAND** | Wildflowers soften part of the rugged coast by the Bedruthan Steps. | *Adam Burton*

ORGAN PIPE NATIONAL MONUMENT, ARIZONA | Yellow petals of Mexican poppies
juxtapose a cholla cactus skeleton. | *Jack Dykinga*

HVERFJALL CRATER, ICELAND | Under a full moon, wind sweeps snow into drifts. | *Orsolya Haarberg*

OPPOSITE: **NEW SOUTH WALES, AUSTRALIA** | In Sydney's North Bondi suburb, multicolored houses crowd a cliff above crashing surf. | *Rune Svendsen*

NEXT PAGES: **ICELAND** | The calm, geothermal waters of the Blue Lagoon match the sky overhead. | *HawaiiBlue*

"The black basaltic rocks that make up the Faroe Islands coastline can overwhelm a photograph, making images feel cold and colorless. But such a dramatic location deserves to be photographed, and fortunately this beautiful little rock pool came to my rescue, a pool of emerald in a dark landscape.

~Adam Burton

EYSTUROY, NORTH ATLANTIC OCEAN | A circle of green rims a rock pool on the shore of Gjógv in the Faroe Islands. | *Adam Burton*

GRAND TETON NATIONAL PARK, WYOMING | Majestic snowcapped peaks
of the Teton Range rise behind the John Moulton barn. | *Russell Burden*

CARLSBAD, CALIFORNIA | Multicolored flowers form a kaleidoscopic field pattern. | *Alex MacLean*

PALOUSE, WASHINGTON | A light dusting of frost tinges colorful hills. | *Chip Phillips*

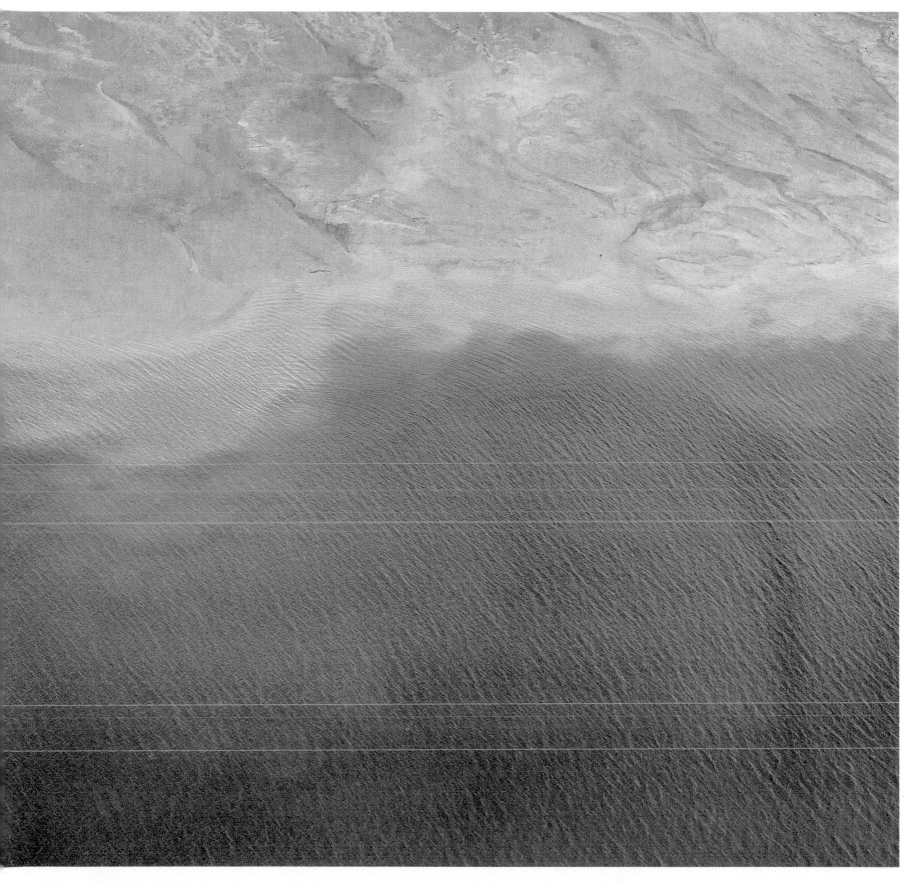

OPPOSITE: **MONUMENT VALLEY, ARIZONA** | Iconic sandstone spires and buttes evoke the American Southwest. | *Chris Van Kan*

PREVIOUS PAGES: **DUBAI, UNITED ARAB EMIRATES** | Turquoise waters ripple into dry land. | *Abrar Mohsin*

The Easter Island seen in photographs is

redolent with mystery, as if of another world.

But when you visit in person, something else takes

over: The figures are the cherished heritage of the

folks living down the road, very real statues of their

ancestors, carved from the island's volcanic stone.

It's very peaceful.

~Jim Richardson

EASTER ISLAND, PACIFIC OCEAN | A path winds past giant *moai* statues that the ancient Rapa Nui built. | *Jim Richardson*

OPPOSITE: LAIKIPIA, KENYA │ Zebras flank a black rhinoceros
under a darkening sky at Solio Ranch. │ *Robin Moore*

NEXT PAGES: MOSTAR, BOSNIA AND HERZEGOVINA │ Lights bathe the
Stari Most, a rebuilt stone bridge over the Neretva River. │ *Oliver Tjaden*

PALOUSE, WASHINGTON | A road cuts a deep path through spring wheat. | *Danita Delimont*

THE NETHERLANDS | Yellow tulips line a flowered path in a wooded garden. | *Paul Nicklen*

IGUAÇU NATIONAL PARK, BRAZIL | Water cascades over
the many cataracts of Iguaçu Falls. | *Frans Lanting*

OPPOSITE: **SNAKE RIVER, WYOMING** | Sunset paints clouds and snow at the headwaters of the Snake River. | *Michael Melford*

NEXT PAGES: **STATE FOREST STATE PARK, COLORADO** | Wildflowers blanket a field in a mountainous Colorado park. | *Art Wolfe*

"Antelope Canyon is one of the most beautiful places I know. The interplay of colors, textures, and light is the masterpiece of a great artist. While the popular Upper Antelope Canyon immediately captures you with its fascinating light beams, Lower Antelope Canyon is subtler. It's not so busy and thus makes for a more intimate experience.

~Andreas Wonisch

ANTELOPE CANYON, ARIZONA | Light accentuates sandstone formations. | *Andreas Wonisch*

SALAR DE UYUNI, BOLIVIA | Salt pyramids punctuate
the Altiplano, high in the Andes. | *Sergio Ballivian*

YUNNAN PROVINCE, CHINA | Eight Tibetan Buddhist stupas align. | *Dong Lei*

LOFOTEN ISLANDS, NORWAY | A rainbow appears over Skrova Island. | *Marcus Bleasdale*

OPPOSITE: GIVERNY, FRANCE | Water lilies float on still pond waters in Claude Monet's garden. | *Diane Cook and Len Jenshel*

NEXT PAGES: MISSION MOUNTAINS, MONTANA | Horses and riders cross stunning scenery in northwestern Montana. | *Keith Ladzinski*

HAKODATE, JAPAN | Blossoming cherry trees cast soft reflections in still water. | *Hiroyuki Morita*

BALI, INDONESIA | A limestone pillar arcs over the water off Nusa Penida Island. | *Jason Edwards*

ZHREBCHEVO LAKE, BULGARIA | Silken waters surround
an old village church. | *Plamen Kojuharov*

I take the majority of my photographs in Poland, during flights within a radius of 60 kilometers from Gdynia, where I live. I want to leave the photographs open for interpretation. It is up to you what you actually see in the photograph—whether it is the dark green shadows of trees or something else entirely.

~Kacper Kowalski

OPPOSITE: **WEJHEROWO, POLAND** | Shadows drape a sculpted golf course near the Baltic coast. | *Kacper Kowalski*

NEXT PAGES: **NAMIB-NAUKLUFT PARK, NAMIBIA** | Graceful springbok walk along the sands and red dunes of the Namib Desert. | *Art Wolfe*

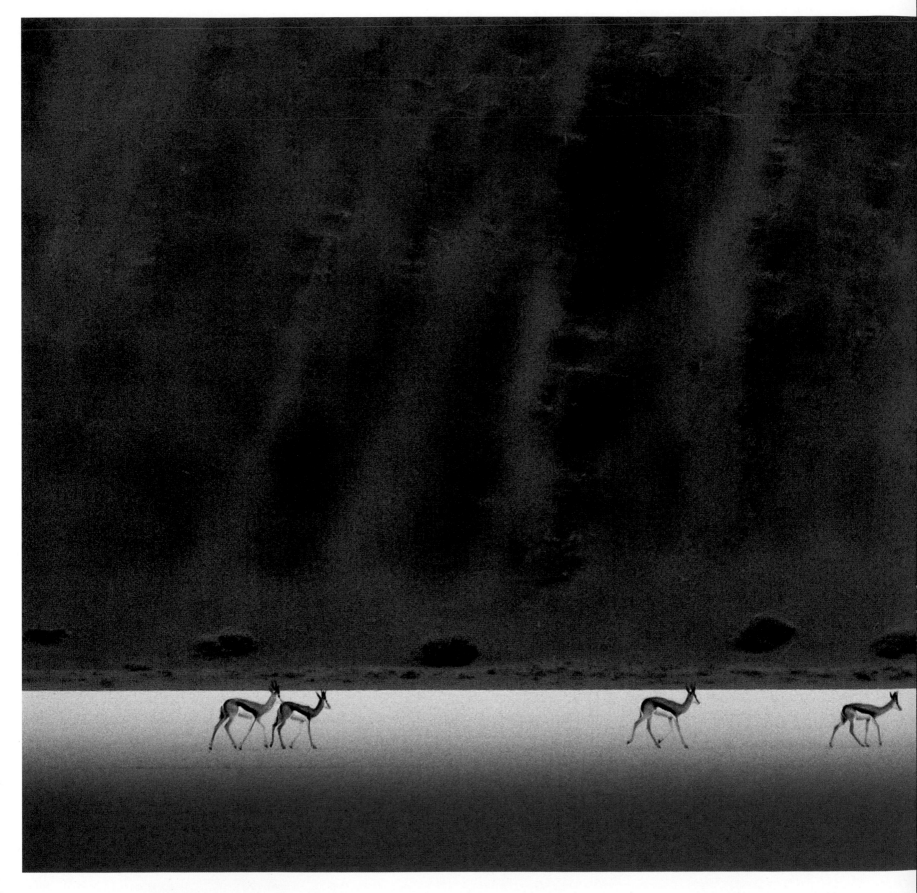

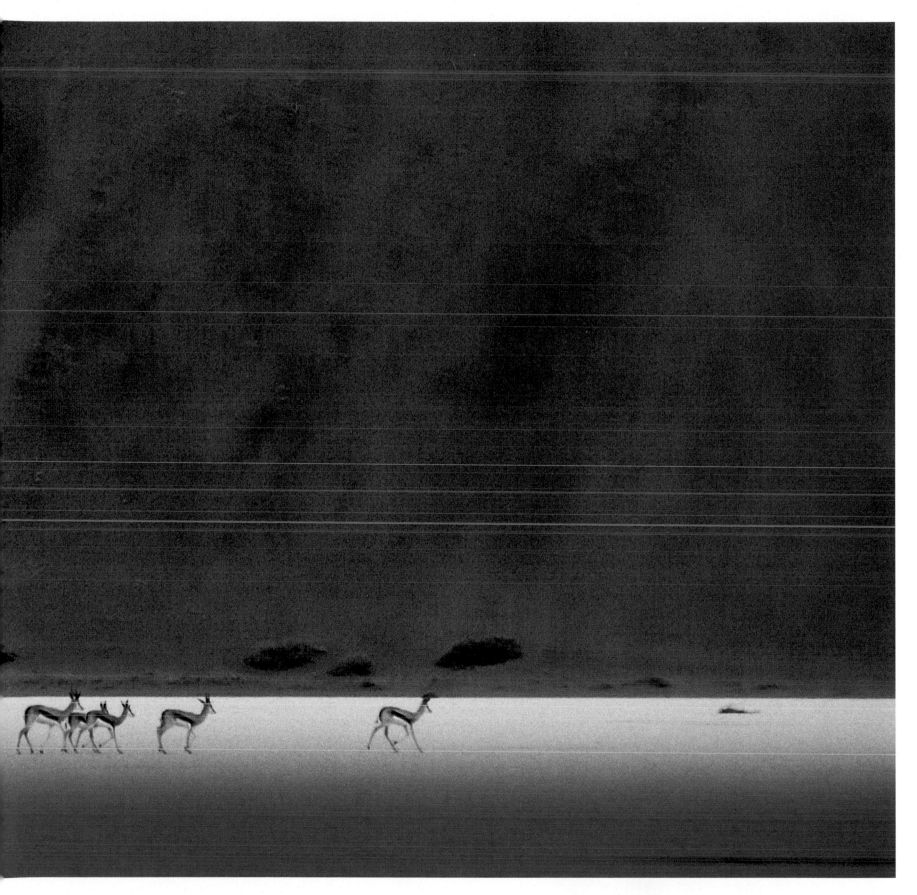

HALLE, BELGIUM | Bluebells carpet a forest floor. | *Waldo Bogaert*

OPPOSITE: **GRAND TETON NATIONAL PARK, WYOMING** |
Sunrise lights the Teton Range before evergreen forests
along the Snake River. | *Keith Ladzinski*

NEXT PAGES: **HITACHI, JAPAN** | Nature seekers walk among hills
full of flowering baby blue eyes. | *Danilo Dungo*

TUSCANY, ITALY | Rolling hills embrace a lone tree on a slope in Volterra, Italy. | *Tino Soriano*

MÅLØY, NORWAY | Waves sculpt Kannesteinen Rock, as they have for thousands of years. | *Nikolay Dimitrov*

NEKO HARBOR, ANTARCTICA | A breeding colony of gentoo penguins
occupies a bare shore. | *David Merron*

VÉZAC, FRANCE | The lush sculptured gardens of Marqueyssac | *Philippe Body*

A storm cleared, and after days of dark
turbulence the polar air was pure and translucent.
Small ice floes covered with a layer of fresh snow
surrounded our sailboat and hit its steel hull, their
impact bringing forth high crystalline sounds
of tiny brass bells.

~Yva Momatiuk and John Eastcott

OPPOSITE: **SOUTH SANDWICH ISLANDS, SOUTH ATLANTIC OCEAN** | Clouds and floating ice center
an Antarctic iceberg. | *Yva Momatiuk and John Eastcott*

NEXT PAGES: **HUNAN PROVINCE, CHINA** | Tree-topped sandstone pillars tower in Wulingyuan Scenic
and Historic Interest Area in central China. | *Thierry Bornier*

90

PROVENCE, FRANCE | Wind sets wheat and lavender in motion. | *Veronika K. Ko*

GIZA, EGYPT | The Pyramids at Giza pierce the sky behind a man leading two camels across amber sands. | *Richard T. Nowitz*

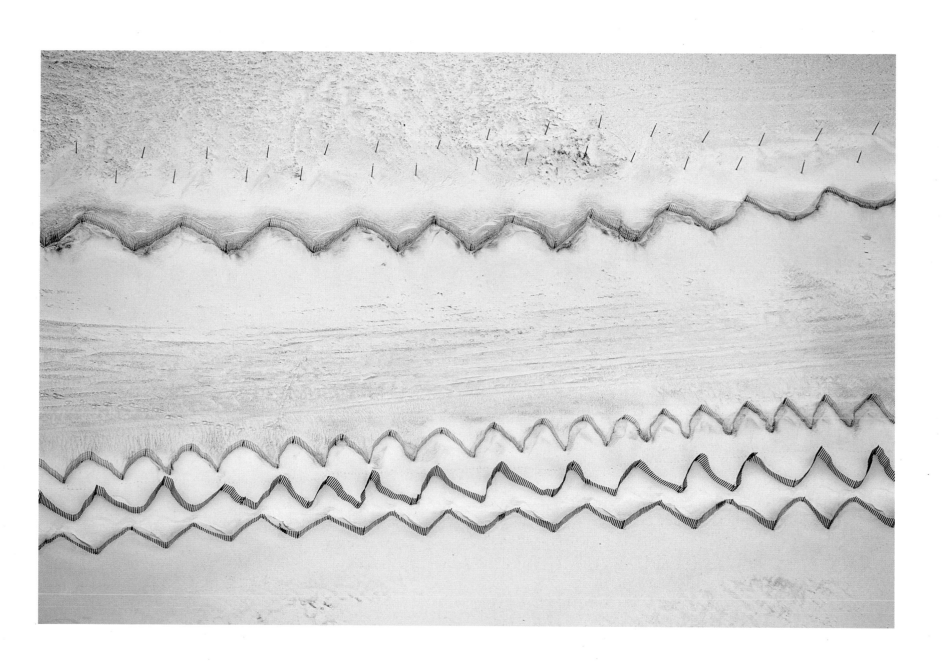

MASTIC BEACH, NEW YORK | Fences zigzag across the shoreline's ivory sands. | *Alex MacLean*

OPPOSITE: **DARTMOOR NATIONAL PARK, ENGLAND** | The moss, ferns, and dwarf oaks of Wistman's Wood harken back to primordial times. | *Duncan George*

PREVIOUS PAGES: **RAJASTHAN, INDIA** | In the early morning birds take flight above the abandoned buildings of Jal Mahal in Jaipur. | *Ravikanth Kurma*

Fog often occurs here, especially in spring and early summer. You need good luck to see a scene this spectacular. After rain this harmonious night view of Mount Fuji appeared. The sea of thick clouds was colored by the lights below. I captured this fantastic scene in a three-minute exposure.

~Takashi

SHIMOTSUMA, JAPAN | Morning fog settles over a field of wildflowers. | *Teruo Araya*

OPPOSITE: **MADAGASCAR, AFRICA** | As the day ends, baobab trees are mirrored in flat waters. | *G&M Therin-Weise*

NEXT PAGES: **SERENGETI NATIONAL PARK, TANZANIA** | Cheetahs survey the Serengeti from a termite mound. | *Frans Lanting*

Ah, *summer,* what power you have to make

us suffer and like it.   ~ Russell Baker

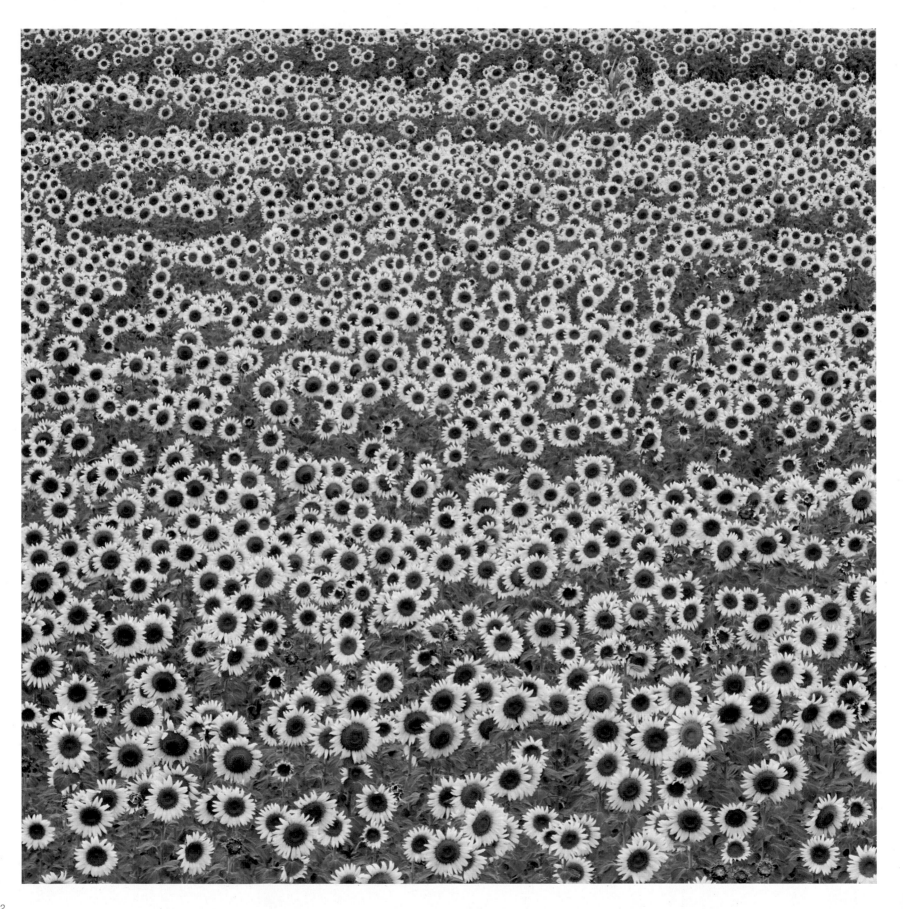

In the middle of a sweet summer day

it feels as if this is how it should be forever. Blue skies, tender breeze, nature at the solstice extreme. At distant latitudes, the warming world turns ice to water.

The sun awakens before we do and stays up past bedtime. The green world stretches into the clear blue sky, catching every ray of light it can. Plants push the limits of how far they grew the year before. Sap courses unseen, up and down and through the trunks, limbs, and branches, each tree's inward flow silently echoing the surge of water through summer landscapes. Flowers show off their most outrageous colors: bright pink, blood red, brash orange, brilliant yellow. Summer can mean abundance. Bouquets turn the pleasures of the season into something we can hold and cherish and give away.

As summer flowers clamor for attention, something even bolder builds up above, and the forces of summer insist we turn our attention to the sky. Afternoon clouds congregate. Their contours mount, dune upon snowy dune. They seem to gain in substance, darkening as they go. The force, the winds, the energy gather, towering over all until with a deafening burst of light and sound and power they release. Thunder follows, rumbles rolling on and on into the vast world beyond our ken.

Emerging from the storm, refreshed by the rain, summer stretches out again. Fruit ripens; fledglings take wing. Grasses bend with the weight of swelling grain. And if we are lucky—if the light slants and the droplets of moisture hang in the balance just so—the sky fills with a million prisms, and for the briefest moment summer skies climax in all the colors of the rainbow.

KANSAS | Bright yellow sunflowers fill a midwestern field. | *Yva Momatiuk and John Eastcott*

OPPOSITE: **INYO NATIONAL FOREST, CALIFORNIA** | Weathered, twisting branches of an ancient bristlecone pine seem to dance. | *Ken Lee*

NEXT PAGES: **KAUAI, HAWAII** | A rainbow over the ruggedly beautiful Na Pali Coast plunges into the Pacific. | *Frans Lanting*

MINNESOTA | Tire tracks leave faint indentions in a lush green field. | *Paul Chesley*

BRITISH COLUMBIA, CANADA | A green islet appears to float
on the waters of Tumuch Lake. | *Shane Kalyn*

LONDON, ENGLAND | A golden sunrise silhouettes a deer herd
in a misty field in Richmond Park. | *Giuseppe Azzena*

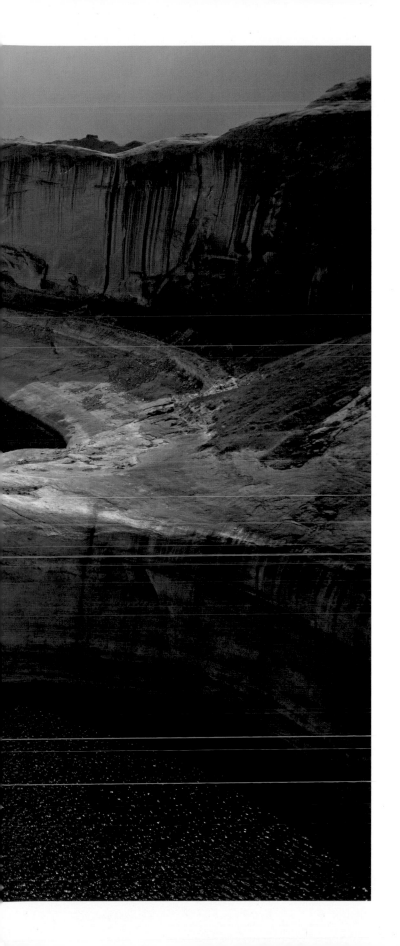

GLEN CANYON NATIONAL RECREATION AREA, UTAH |
A motorboat rides the gentle curves of Reflection Canyon. | *Michael Melford*

"The hike up to the Col Raiser alpine pastures from Selva di Val Gardena rewards you with stunning views of the hand-cut grass fields, looking eastward toward the dominating peaks of the Geisler group. This pasture suddenly drops away on the northern edge into the valley below.

~James Buchan

OPPOSITE: SELVA DI VAL GARDENA, ITALY | An angled meadow in the Italian Dolomites | James Buchan

NEXT PAGES: YANGSHUO, CHINA | Cone-shaped karst peaks stretch to the horizon in early morning. | Karl Willson

DEAD SEA, ISRAEL | Tourists at the Ein Bokek resort wade into the Dead Sea's buoyant waters. | *George Steinmetz*

DUXBURY, MASSACHUSETTS | Colorful dinghies cluster around a dock. | *Alex MacLean*

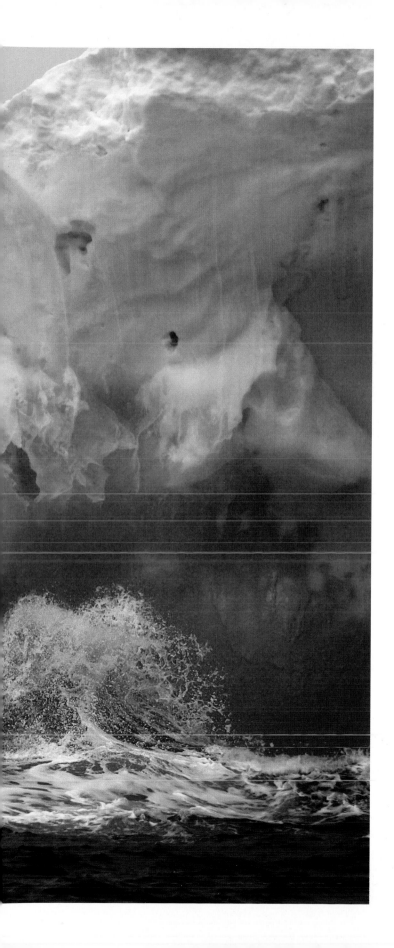

SOUTH SANDWICH ISLANDS, SOUTH ATLANTIC OCEAN | A circular hole in a striking blue
iceberg appears like a portal leading to an icy realm. | *Maria Stenzel*

OPPOSITE: **GREAT WALL OF CHINA, JINSHANLING SECTION** | The defensive walls of China's fortress masterpiece stretch along verdant, green hills. | *Martos Hoffman*

NEXT PAGES: **OIA, GREECE** | A brilliant orange sunset adds to the glimmer from the homes of the Mediterranean's Santorini island. | *Inge Johnsson*

"On this morning I hiked about a mile into the aspen grove at Kebler Pass and was completely alone. The grove stretches for miles, and these lush, green plants reach up to about six feet. While the forest is a very different place depending on the season, it's always spectacular, wild, and open.

~Keith Ladzinski

NEAR CRESTED BUTTE, COLORADO | White aspens highlight the rich green undergrowth in a forest glen. | *Keith Ladzinski*

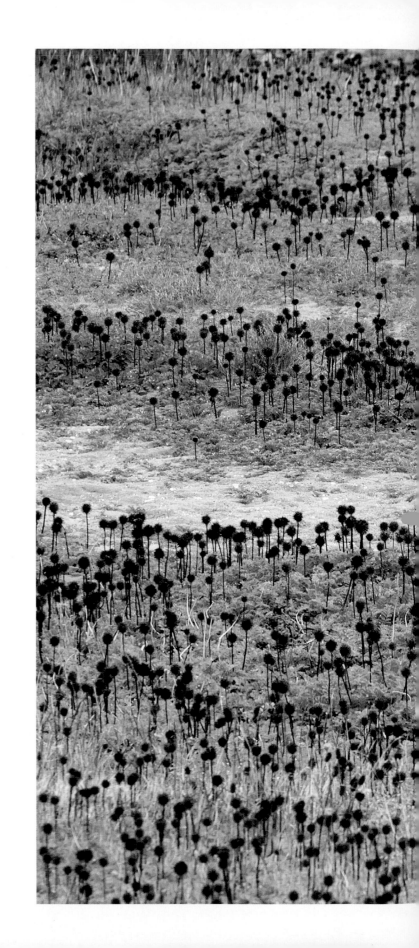

SOUTH GEORGIA, SOUTH ATLANTIC OCEAN | Greater burnet wildflowers enliven
the tundra near Stromness whaling station. | *Michael Melford*

GULF OF ALASKA | Burgundy algae and ribbons of lighter sedges and grasses fork across the mudflats surrounding Cook Inlet. | *Art Wolfe*

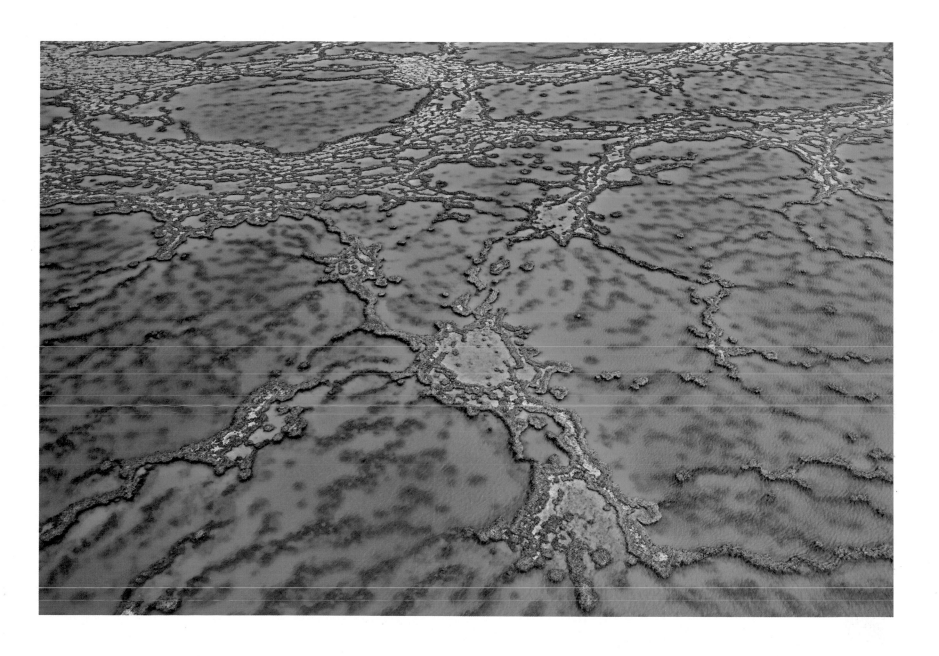

GREAT BARRIER REEF, AUSTRALIA | Coral on the Hardy Reef
forms cellular patterns. | *Ingo Arndt*

OPPOSITE: **VANCOUVER ISLAND, CANADA** | Tadpoles swim through a lily pad forest in Cedar Lake. | *Eiko Jones*

PREVIOUS PAGES: **SVALBARD, NORWAY** | A polar bear steps along Arctic pack ice. | *Ralph Lee Hopkins*

QUANZHOU, CHINA | Sunbeams light a forest path for a woman carrying buckets. | *Tianyi Liu*

NORFOLK, ENGLAND | Day draws to a close at the dunes along Holkam Bay. | *Jon Gibbs*

"The view from this cliff-top vista resembles a scene from science fiction. If you don't notice the road passing through the valley, it feels like a thousand years ago when these bizarre monasteries were home to monks or nuns who isolated themselves from the outside world by living on top of giant, sandstone pillars.

~Babak Tafreshi

OPPOSITE: **THESSALY, GREECE** | Monasteries on the sandstone pillars of Meteora, a World Heritage site | *Babak Tafreshi*

NEXT PAGES: **PALOUSE, WASHINGTON** | Golden grain fields seem to match the color of distant honey-yellow hills. | *Chip Phillips*

ANTONIO VARAS PENINSULA, CHILE | Four *bagualeros*—cowboys—pause their search for feral livestock against Patagonia's stunning backdrop. | *Tomás Munita*

GEORGIA, UNITED STATES | Spanish moss drapes twisted branches
of live oaks that shade a quiet lane. | *Maria Stenzel*

TOGIAK NATIONAL WILDLIFE REFUGE, ALASKA | The Igushik River forms a ribbon of brilliant blue as it flows south to Nushagak Bay. | *Michael Melford*

"This is a deeply layered place, where you step back into ancient times on volcanic basalt columns laid 60 million years ago, where relentless waves claw day and night, and where mythical Irish giant Finn McCool built his causeway. Here you may indulge whatever level of scientific reason or mystical magic that makes your heart glad.

~Jim Richardson

OPPOSITE: **GIANT'S CAUSEWAY, NORTHERN IRELAND** | Waves splash against polygon-shaped volcanic rocks. | *Jim Richardson*

PREVIOUS PAGES: **PORT CAMPBELL NATIONAL PARK, AUSTRALIA** | A soft summer sky illuminates the giant limestone pillars known as the Twelve Apostles. | *Stoneography*

OPPOSITE: **PENÍNSULA DE GUANAHACABIBES BIOSPHERE RESERVE, CUBA** | A distant sailboat and a puffy white cloud add to the Caribbean Sea's tranquility. | *Steve Winter*

NEXT PAGES: **MOUNT HOOD, OREGON** | Wildfire smoke envelops the Cascade Range as seen from a weathered whitebark pine's perch on Mound Hood. | *Paul C. Glasser*

ROCKPORT, MASSACHUSETTS | A red fishing shack proudly wears
an American flag on the New England coast. | *Stan Tess*

SOUTH GOBI, MONGOLIA | A double rainbow makes a stunning panorama for yurts in the foreground. | *Ira Block*

LAKE NAM, CHINA | Prayer flags stretch toward a high altitude lake on the Tibetan Plateau. | *Michael S. Yamashita*

EVERGLADES NATIONAL PARK, FLORIDA | Salt-loving mangroves
punctuate still waters as sky and water merge at day's end. | *Mac Stone*

"When I entered the blooming lavender fields of Valensole in French Provence, I was struck by a crazy perfume of lavender flowers covering the ground from one horizon to the other. Purple hills of flowering rows alternate with green hills of already cut lavender. It's an astonishing view that everyone should see in a lifetime.

~Vadim Balakin

OPPOSITE: **PROVENCE, FRANCE** | Parallel rows of lavender and vibrant pink clouds compose a surreal vista of the Valensole Plateau. | *Vadim Balakin*

NEXT PAGES: **LIGURIA, ITALY** | Beach umbrellas make a colorful mosaic over the sands of Monterosso al Mare on the Italian Riviera. | *H. P. Huber*

NEAR GREELEY, COLORADO | A dirt road intersects strips of green fields. | *Paul Chesley*

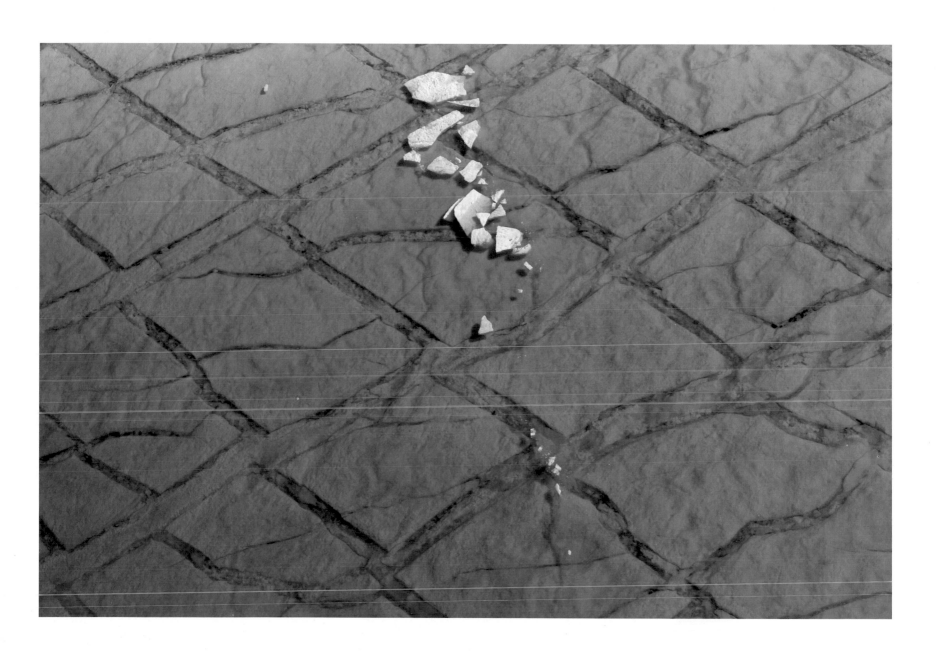

GREENLAND | As if tossed randomly, white ice drifts
on the surface of a meltwater lake. | *Daniel Beltrá*

GREAT SAND DUNES NATIONAL PARK AND PRESERVE, COLORADO | Climbers
shrink from view as they ascend the tallest dunes in North America. | *Barbara Motter*

"I love the Orcia Valley because of its gently overlapping hills, which are usually covered with a smooth fog in the moments right before sunrise. On this morning all was silent while I used a wide-angle lens to capture these pink, soft clouds.

~Maurizio Rellini

OPPOSITE: **TUSCANY, ITALY** | Dawn comes to the Orcia Valley. | *Maurizio Rellini*

NEXT PAGES: **MACHU PICCHU, PERU** | High in the Andes, clouds hover above the pre-Columbian Inca city of Machu Picchu. | *Jim Richardson*

NORMANDY, FRANCE | Mont Saint-Michel twinkles as twilight descends
on the bay surrounding the medieval monastery. | *bluejayphoto*

OPPOSITE: **MALDIVES, INDIAN OCEAN** | Glistening blue water, white sands, and green palm trees complete an iconic beach scene. | *Martin Child*

NEXT PAGES: **CASCADE RANGE, WASHINGTON** | *Wildflower patches and verdant slopes roll toward Mount Rainier's snowcapped volcanic peak.* | *Art Wolfe*

ICELAND | Water tumbles over Háifoss and Granni waterfalls. | *Orsolya Haarberg*

YUCATÁN, MEXICO | A sunbeam spotlights a swimmer in the Xkeken cenote, which the Maya believed led to the underworld. | *John Stanmeyer*

EXMOOR, ENGLAND | Ponies graze in fields of heather. | *Adam Burton*

OKAYAMA PREFECTURE, JAPAN | Fireflies form blinking rivers
of light in a still woodland. | *Trevor Williams*

" I took this picture in 2015, on the hottest day of the summer. I was sweating away in my plane. Many images are taken during the day's corners, when the shadows get longer, but people aren't bathing then. So I used a long telephoto lens and took this picture from quite far away to capture the structure and form.

~Hans Blossey

HALTERN AM SEE, GERMANY | Beachgoers take their place on the crowded sand. | *Hans Blossey*

EBERGÖTZEN, GERMANY | A flock of geese huddles close in rain. | *Gerd Ludwig*

IVVAVIK NATIONAL PARK, CANADA | Dandelions shift with the wind. | *Michael Melford*

OPPOSITE: **BORA BORA, FRENCH POLYNESIA** | A barrier reef curves around craggy Mount Otemanu. | *Frans Lanting*

NEXT PAGES: **SARHADD, AFGHANISTAN** | A field of wildflowers contrasts rugged mountains. | *Matthieu Paley*

Autumn is a second spring when every

AUT

Autumn is a second spring when every leaf is a flower. ~ Albert Camus

Just as there is wisdom in aging, so there is beauty in the fall. No other

season reminds us so vividly of the passage of time, the intensity of loss, the need to find meaning in absence.

Dry grasses rustle; greens fade into yellow and brown; trees sigh and submit their leaves to the passing gusts of wind. Watch one leaf as it drifts through the air. Its crinkled edges like misshapen ailerons, it rocks wearily like a skiff in broad ocean swells. Watch that leaf as it falls. Let it go; let it go.

Autumn is such a fickle season. It taunts us with its vibrant hues. Cherry red, lemon yellow, peachy orange: up in the forest treetops and down under, in a coral world elsewhere on the globe. The landscape glows again with a challenge to the year's earlier pleasures. After the flowers, the fruit, the rainbow—now our spirits soar; once again we get the chance to revel in color. Once again we celebrate nature's infinite cycles.

Yet autumn is a stern teacher. It has lessons to tell us amid this chaos of color. Seek to distinguish between what to preserve and what to leave behind. Gather the fruits of the full year's labors. Thankfully harvest. Take note of what deserves special attention in the dwindling of the light.

Evening grows golden, closing in on the hours of the day. The sun's warmth lulls us for a while, and then the weather snaps. Frost filigrees the morning. Indian summer, they call this last spate of warm weather, but no one seems to know quite why. Hunting weather? Final harvest? Or simply communion with the open air of the natural world before the time for hunkering down.

OPPOSITE: **VIENNA, AUSTRIA** | Groomed trees form an archway of green and orange over a pedestrian walkway. | *Dmytrii Minishev*

NEXT PAGES: **ANGLESEY, WALES** | A sandy path leads to a lookout tower on Llanddwyn Island. | *Adam Burton*

GRAND STAIRCASE-ESCALANTE NATIONAL MONUMENT, UTAH |
A lone cottonwood tree finds purchase in a depression in smooth, red rock. | *Guy Tal*

PAMUKKALE, TURKEY | Thermal waters held in travertine terraces catch the last rays of sunlight. | *Jan Wlodarczyk*

VICTORIA FALLS, ZAMBIA AND ZIMBABWE | The rushing waters of Victoria Falls
cascade into the Zambezi River. | *Annie Griffiths*

LAKE MANYARA NATIONAL PARK, TANZANIA | Green growth thrives in a deep gorge near Lake Manyara in the East African Rift Valley system. | *Ralph Lee Hopkins*

OPPOSITE: **KIMBE BAY, PAPUA NEW GUINEA** | A father and son fish from an outrigger canoe above colorful corals, which thrive in the reef system off New Britain. | *David Doubilet*

NEXT PAGES: **SAN FRANCISCO, CALIFORNIA** | A span of the Golden Gate Bridge peeks above low-hanging morning fog. | *Dave Gordon*

XINJIANG UYGUR AUTONOMOUS REGION, CHINA | Yellow tufts of trees
poke out of the sands of the Taklimakan dune field. | *George Steinmetz*

223

OPPOSITE: **HOKKAIDO, JAPAN** | October snowfall dusts trees and autumn leaves overhanging an emerald green pond. | *Kent Shiraishi*

NEXT PAGES: **BAVARIA, GERMANY** | Neuschwanstein Castle gleams in the late afternoon light. | *Walter Bibikow*

KALYMNOS, GREECE | During an early October sunset, a cave's archway
frames a view over Panormos village. | *Peter Holly*

RAPA ITI, FRENCH POLYNESIA | Sharks languidly swim in the South Pacific waters surrounding sparsely populated Rapa Iti. | *Manu San Felix*

"We had spent most of the afternoon fighting the wind to get a good oblique angle on the "Spiral Jetty" and were low on fuel when I asked the pilot to make one tight doughnut turn over the top. As the small helicopter wheeled on its side, I hung out the door and peered straight down. This was the last shot.

~George Steinmetz

GREAT SALT LAKE, UTAH | A lingering drought reveals the salt-encrusted spirals of Robert Smithson's artwork "Spiral Jetty," at Rozel Point peninsula. | *George Steinmetz*

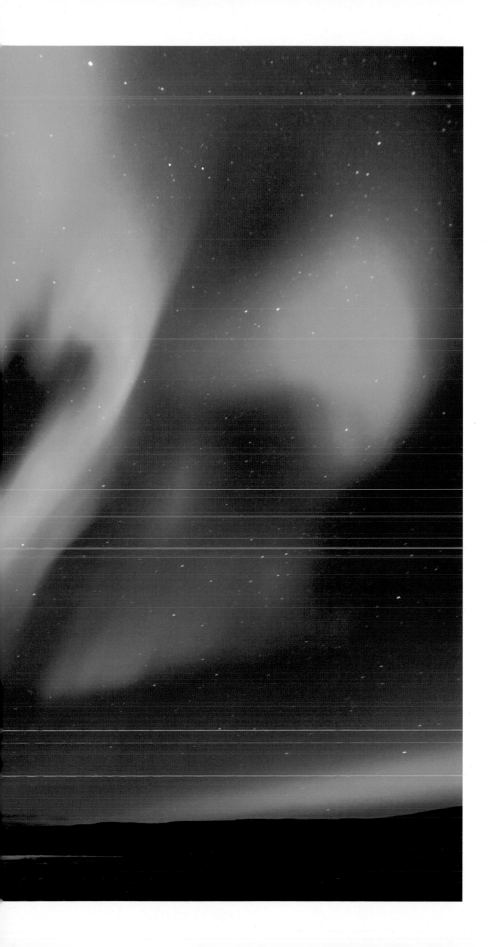

BREIÐAVÍK, ICELAND | The aurora borealis creates vibrant green spectral
shapes in the dark sky above an Icelandic church. | *G. Petkov*

COLUMBIA RIVER GORGE, OREGON | Golden trees and a rushing stream
create a quintessential fall forest scene. | *Marc Adamus*

NAMIB-NAUKLUFT PARK, NAMIBIA | In Deadvlei, a camel thorn tree
stands tall underneath a star-studded sky. | *Beth McCarley*

ATTICA, GREECE | Sunset falls on the Temple of Poseidon,
just as it has for nearly 2,500 years. | *Orestis Panagiotou*

EMILIA-ROMAGNA, ITALY | Calm waters reflect the slender trunks of wispy trees. | *dpellicola*

" I got up before dawn to hike out to

Lake Matheson to photograph the New Zealand

Alps reflected in its waters. Walking back to my car,

I noticed such nice light on the trees that I stopped

and took this picture. The moral of the story is:

Never walk past a picture.

~Michael Melford

OPPOSITE: WESTLAND TAI POUTINI NATIONAL PARK, NEW ZEALAND | The rising sun sheds soft light on trees
near Lake Matheson on the west coast of New Zealand's South Island. | *Michael Melford*

PREVIOUS PAGES: YUNNAN PROVINCE, CHINA | The region's red soil and green cultivated fields create a tapestry
unfurling amid rugged hillsides. | *Thierry Bornier*

242

OPPOSITE: **ALBANY, AUSTRALIA** | A pelican leaves a solitary wake in Princess Royal Harbour. | *Jason Edwards*

NEXT PAGES: **PENNINE ALPS, ITALY-SWITZERLAND** | The Matterhorn's summit glows red with the sun. | *Alessandra Meniconzi*

RIOMAGGIORE, ITALY | Multicolored houses spill down a cliffside in an Italian village beneath a blushing October sky. | *Stefano Politi Markovina*

NAMIB-NAUKLUFT PARK, NAMIBIA | Burnt-orange dunes reach hundreds
of feet upward in the southern Namib Desert. | *Andrei Duman*

ACADIA NATIONAL PARK, MAINE | Red leaves against gray, speckled bark | *Michael Melford*

ULURU-KATA TJUTA NATIONAL PARK, AUSTRALIA | Uluru glows in the middle
of the Australian outback. | *Art Wolfe*

> " The division of Central Park's saturated foliage and Manhattan's incredible architecture is comprehended in an entirely different way in this bird's-eye view. Aerial photography offers a wondrous change in perspective, evoking new emotions from the views seen on foot. I captured this on my first helicopter flight over Manhattan, a birthday gift I'll never forget!
>
> ~Kayte Dolmatch

OPPOSITE: **CENTRAL PARK, NEW YORK CITY** | Central Park West divides park from buildings. | *Kayte Dolmatch*

PREVIOUS PAGES: **JASPER NATIONAL PARK, CANADA** | The Athabasca River meanders through foliage at the foot of the Canadian Rockies. | *Marc Adamus*

OPPOSITE: **CORTES BANKS, PACIFIC OCEAN** | A sheepshead fish (foreground) and senorita fish swim through a kelp forest. | *Brian Skerry*

NEXT PAGES: **KOGGALA, SRI LANKA** | Fishermen perched on stilts wait for the fish to bite in the Laccadive Sea. | *Kimberley Coole*

DEATH VALLEY NATIONAL PARK, CALIFORNIA | Veins of salt give texture
to the salt flats of Badwater Basin. | *Michael Melford*

GOÐAFOSS, ICELAND | Milky-white waters of an Icelandic waterfall
are a dramatic backdrop for a moss-covered stone. | *Orsolya Haarberg*

YUKON, CANADA | Azure Lake, formed by glacial meltwater, punctuates the rugged Ogilvie Mountains with a splash of blue. | *Paul Nicklen*

OPPOSITE: GUANGXI ZHUANG AUTONOMOUS REGION, CHINA | Moon Hill's arch dwarfs a climber. | *Carsten Peter*

PREVIOUS PAGES: TORRES DEL PAINE NATIONAL PARK, CHILE | Autumn in Patagonia brings a palette of blue water and golden grasses. | *Yva Momatiuk and John Eastcott*

MADEIRA, PORTUGAL | Falling water evokes tranquillity
at Monte Palace Tropical Garden. | *Zoltan Duray*

" It was a cloudy and foggy day in a magical forest of cork oaks and ferns. Among the fallen leaves were two huge parasol mushrooms. It was a mysterious place, forgotten, with an autumnal atmosphere. The wide angle magnified the mushrooms in that foggy environment.

~Andrés Miguel Domínguez

OPPOSITE: LOS ALCORNOCALES NATURAL PARK, SPAIN | In a foggy woodland, parasol mushrooms point up toward the surrounding cork oak trees. | *Andrés Miguel Domínguez*

NEXT PAGES: PALOUSE, WASHINGTON | Harvested wheat takes a luminous glow from the setting sun. | *Chip Phillips*

KUNMING, CHINA | Intricate rock formations of the Naigu Stone Forest | *Carsten Peter*

DEATH VALLEY NATIONAL PARK, CALIFORNIA | The Joshua trees of Lee Flat
appear washed out in a November sky. | *Michael Melford*

GATES OF THE ARCTIC NATIONAL PARK AND PRESERVE, ALASKA | Poplar tree groves
line a gilded tundra. | *Michael Melford*

PEŞTERA, ROMANIA | Frosted tree branches and grasses transform the countryside. | *Eduard Gutescu*

" I climbed on a rocky hill under one of the hottest suns in the world to get this picture, but the view was worth the effort. It is one of the best places to see Nabataean graves in the Middle East. The moment was surreal: no human noise or engine noise, just tombs to the horizon.

~Eric Lafforgue

OPPOSITE: **MADAIN SALIH, SAUDI ARABIA** | Carved into rock, ancient Nabataean tombs echo centuries past. | *Eric Lafforgue*

PREVIOUS PAGES: **GLACIER BAY NATIONAL PARK AND PRESERVE, ALASKA** | Fog streams through the blue-tinted Lamplugh Glacier. | *Michael Melford*

SLEEPY HOLLOW, NEW YORK | Night's stillness surrounds gardens at Kykuit, the John D. Rockefeller Estate. | *Diane Cook and Len Jenshel*

XINJIANG UYGUR AUTONOMOUS REGION, CHINA | A bird's-eye view of a village
in Fuyun Xian | *George Steinmetz*

MUDDUS NATIONAL PARK, SWEDEN | Clear blue lake waters
mirror the cloud-filled sky. | *Orsolya Haarberg*

OPPOSITE: **NAMBUNG NATIONAL PARK, AUSTRALIA** | The limestone spires of Western Australia's Pinnacles Desert cast long shadows at sunrise. | *Kyle Hammons*

PREVIOUS PAGES: **EDELSTAL, AUSTRIA** | Windmills stand tall in the wine fields of Burgenland. | *Matej Ková*

" The tiny Pacific City, and the looming sandstone bluff that is Cape Kiwanda, make this area one of my favorite places to photograph. This image was shot out on the very tip of the cape at sunrise. There is no better place to take in the morning light and listen to the ocean waves crash up and down the sandstone cliffs.

~Chip Phillips

CAPE KIWANDA STATE NATURAL AREA, OREGON | Sunrise paints sky and sandstone in pink tones. | *Chip Phillips*

ZARAGOZA, SPAIN | Autumn replaces greens with oranges in Moncayo Natural Park. | *David Santiago Garcia*

DORSET, ENGLAND | Well-worn steps lead to the limestone arch
known as the Durdle Door. | *Adam Burton*

SAN JUAN DEL SUR, NICARAGUA | A grass-covered patio overlooks
the crescent-shaped bay of San Juan del Sur. | *Pablo Castagnola*

OPPOSITE: **LAGOS, PORTUGAL** | The rugged coastline of the Algarve
meets the mighty Atlantic. | *Stephen Emerson*

NEXT PAGES: **BALI, INDONESIA** | Storm clouds contrast the striking green
of the Jatiluwih Rice Terraces. | *Jim Richardson*

In seed time learn, in harvest teach, in

winter enjoy. ~ William Blake

The spinning world of winter skimps on daylight. It leans away from the

sun. The light grows thin; it does not warm us; it does not last. Against night's blackness the stars shine cold and distant. On the occasional night when the full moon lights up fresh-fallen snow, we marvel at the emptiness of winter. Oh silent night. All is calm; nothing stirs.

Winter forces survival mode. The world is cold, harsh, and barren. A few green wisps, the occasional risky flower opens. Ice grips the local flow of water. Even the ocean, ceaseless waves upon the shore, shivers with the chill. We emulate the wild ones who hibernate or wing their way toward warmth. We manage in the faith that things will get better.

The ancient Greeks took winter as the time when Hades held his youthful wife hostage in the underworld. Darkness reigned. No crops grew. But the Romans turned that myth on its head, declaring the depths of winter a time for pranks and feasts and frivolity celebrating Saturn, the primeval god of time, overseer of the cycles of birth and death, planting and harvest, abundance and decline. During the Saturnalia, disorder triumphs, and the master serves the slave.

We light candles, sing carols, huddle closer together. We search the empty landscape for what remains. Delicate crystals of ice and snow catch and carry the least little glimmer. Bare of leaves and clutter, the land shows its contours: Earth's lines and curves and intersections now naked, solid, and strong. Dainty footprints in the snow precede us, reminding us that even amid the freeze we can skid and frolic and feel free. A snow-white palette stretches before us, ready for the colors of the coming year.

STIRLINGSHIRE, SCOTLAND | Trees in a winter field hold a soft dusting of snow. | *Robert Fulton*

DEAD SEA, ISRAEL-JORDAN | Sunrise brings a blush of light above odd-shaped salt crystal formations in the Dead Sea. | *Ido Meirovich*

OPPOSITE: **PITZTAL GLACIER, AUSTRIA** | A skier takes flight above an ice cave nearly 10,000 feet high in the Alps. | *Christoph Jorda*

NEXT PAGES: **VENICE, ITALY** | Gondolas wait in the calm waters in front of the church of San Giorgio Maggiore. | *Jim Richardson*

TRANGDALEN, NORWAY | A strip of snow and light
interrupts winter's blue tapestry. | *Michael S. Yamashita*

SAN GABRIEL MOUNTAINS, CALIFORNIA | The setting sun creates a starburst above 9,407-foot Mount Baden-Powell. | *Matthew Kuhns*

"This water-bound willow on Lake Wanaka's southern shore is world famous. It's photographed by millions, but no two shots are the same. The seasons transform both tree and mountains from the rich greens, blues, and browns seen in the summer to the deep pink and red tones of winter.

~Paul Reiffer

CENTRAL OTAGO, NEW ZEALAND | Lake Wanaka's clear waters reflect a lone willow. | *Paul Reiffer*

WHITE SANDS NATIONAL MONUMENT, NEW MEXICO | Snow dusts sand dunes as a yucca
cactus showcases life's vibrancy in the Chihuahuan Desert. | *Russell Burden*

OPPOSITE: ARCHES NATIONAL PARK, UTAH | Sunset brings a red blush
to the weathered sandstone of Delicate Arch. | *Chip Phillips*

PREVIOUS PAGES: JAVA, INDONESIA | Soft morning light brightens the milky clouds that fill the valley
below the Tengger caldera of Bromo-Tengger-Semeru National Park. | *Kyle Hammons*

SALZKAMMERGUT LAKE REGION, AUSTRIA | The sun tops Alpine mountains
to cast light on the village of Hallstatt. | *Harald Nachtmann*

" It was quiet and calm in the airplane—

a magnificent morning flying over Lake Powell,

heading toward Bryce Canyon. The clear blue

of the sky matched the water, and the low lake level

revealed the sublime contrast of red-rock formations.

Look at all this beauty that we humans

are a tiny part of.

~Jassen Todorov

OPPOSITE: ARIZONA | Lake Powell's cerulean waters encircle sandstone. | *Jassen Todorov*

NEXT PAGES: OYMYAKON, RUSSIA | Reindeer on the move | *Dean Conger*

VALDIVIAN COASTAL RESERVE, CHILE | A rainbow arcs over coastal grasses in a temperate forest. | *Ian Shive*

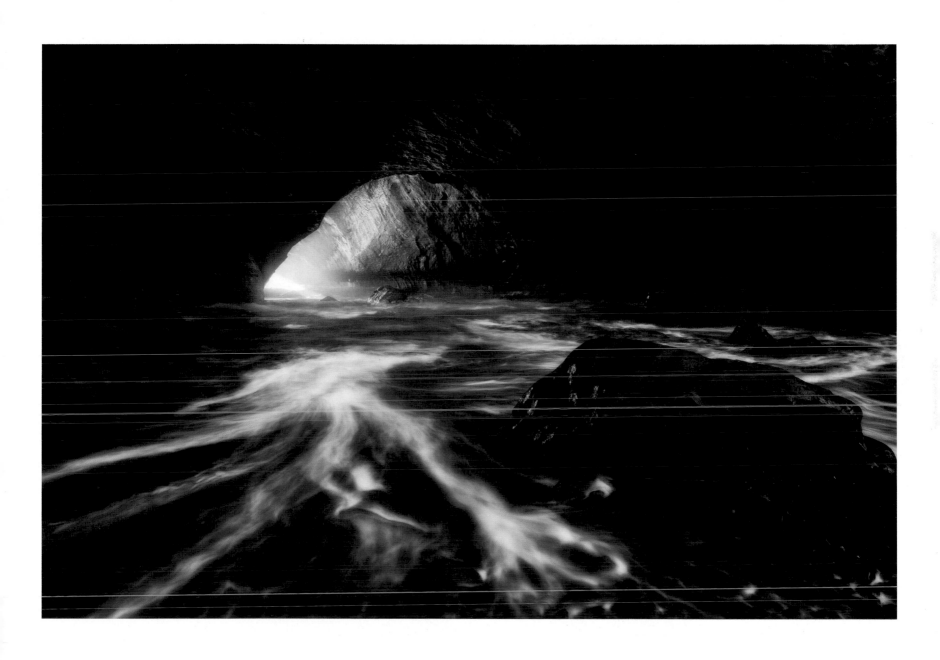

CAPE KIWANDA, OREGON | A coastal sea cave's entrance glows gold
when the sun sets at the right angle. | *Miles Morgan*

OPPOSITE: **BLACK FOREST, GERMANY** | Snow clings to the branches of a tree on the Schauinsland. | *Norbert Rosing*

NEXT PAGES: **SAMUEL H. BOARDMAN STATE SCENIC CORRIDOR, OREGON** | Warm colors contrast the rugged Oregon coast. | *Chip Phillips*

OPPOSITE: **THE KIMBERLEY, WESTERN AUSTRALIA** | A river snakes its way through dense mangrove forest. | *Ralph Lee Hopkins*

NEXT PAGES, LEFT: **TULUM, MEXICO** | A diver hovers between tree branches in a cenote. | *Fabrice Guérin*

NEXT PAGES, RIGHT: **KARNATAKA, INDIA** | Dusk silhouettes the shrine to Hanuman, the Hindu monkey god, on Hemakuta Hill. | *Murali Balasundaram*

HAWAII VOLCANOES NATIONAL PARK, HAWAII | Lava meets
the Pacific Ocean. | *Stephen Alvarez*

NIENHAGEN, GERMANY | Light snow falls in the quiet Gespensterwald,
or Ghost Forest. | *Sandra Bartocha*

"I took this shot on the first day of 2015. The first light was magical. I had been chasing the weather every day, and after dozens of times I caught the moment when nature embraced the Sheikh Zayed Grand Mosque to create this rare scene with the mosque's shadows reflecting over the fog.

~Khalid Al Hammadi

OPPOSITE: **ABU DHABI, UNITED ARAB EMIRATES** | Sheikh Zayed Grand Mosque peeks over fog on New Year's Day. | *Khalid Al Hammadi*

NEXT PAGES: **BANFF NATIONAL PARK, CANADA** | Canadian Rockies overlook glassy Moraine Lake. | *Adam Burton*

OSA PENINSULA, COSTA RICA | Red *Aphelandra lingua-bovis* flowers add color to the green of a rain forest. | *Tim Laman*

VANCOUVER, CANADA | Red umbrellas dangle from bare tree branches
as part of an art installation. | *Andy Clark*

NEW BRUNSWICK, CANADA | Snow blankets Le Pays de la Sagouine,
an Acadian theme park in Bouctouche. | *Hemis*

BERNINA PASS, SWITZERLAND | Snowy scenery dwarfs the *Bernina Express* as it journeys through the Swiss Alps. | *Federica Violin*

OPPOSITE: YELLOWSTONE NATIONAL PARK, WYOMING | In the heart of a Yellowstone winter, two bison make their way across Lion Geyser. | *Norbert Rosing*

PREVIOUS PAGES: DRY TORTUGAS NATIONAL PARK, GULF OF MEXICO. | Gentle surf meets the shore of Garden Key, one of the seven small islands that make up the Dry Tortugas. | *Paul Marcellini*

BADEN-WURTTEMBERG, GERMANY | A Christmas market nestled
in the Black Forest | *Jean-Daniel Sudres*

OPPOSITE: **EMPTY QUARTER, ARABIAN PENINSULA** | A solitary tree's greenery pops amid the sand dunes in the Rub al Khali, or "quarter of emptiness." | *Daniel Schoenen*

PREVIOUS PAGES: **CAPPADOCIA, TURKEY** | Hot air balloons decorate the sky above snowcapped fairy chimneys. | *Murat Oner Tas*

" Mono Lake's landscape is unlike any other
with its alkaline waters and tufa towers. Winter's
dry desert weather produced a subtlety in the lake's
mood, seen in the convergence of soft light, clouds,
and reflections in the water's oil-like surface.
It feels like a land untouched by time.

~Mark Lissick

OPPOSITE: **MONO LAKE, CALIFORNIA** | A tufa tower appears as a castle sprung from the waters of Mono Lake. | *Mark Lissick*

NEXT PAGES: **ICELAND** | Cold Icelandic waters catch the aurora borealis's iridescence. | *Thierry Bornier*

ROCKY MOUNTAINS, CANADA | A stand of snow-draped evergreen trees
casts long shadows across the Canadian Rockies. | *Pete McBride*

ANTARCTICA | An icebreaker opens a trail in its wake. | *Frans Lanting*

YUNNAN PROVINCE, CHINA | Terraced rice fields create a multicolored pattern. | *Thierry Bornier*

OPPOSITE: **VARANGER PENINSULA, NORWAY** | A red fox treads on snow. | *Erlend Haarberg*

NEXT PAGES: **JAMMU AND KASHMIR, INDIA** | At 14,000 feet, the Shanti Stupa,
a peace pagoda, shines in the night over the district of Leh. | *Art Wolfe*

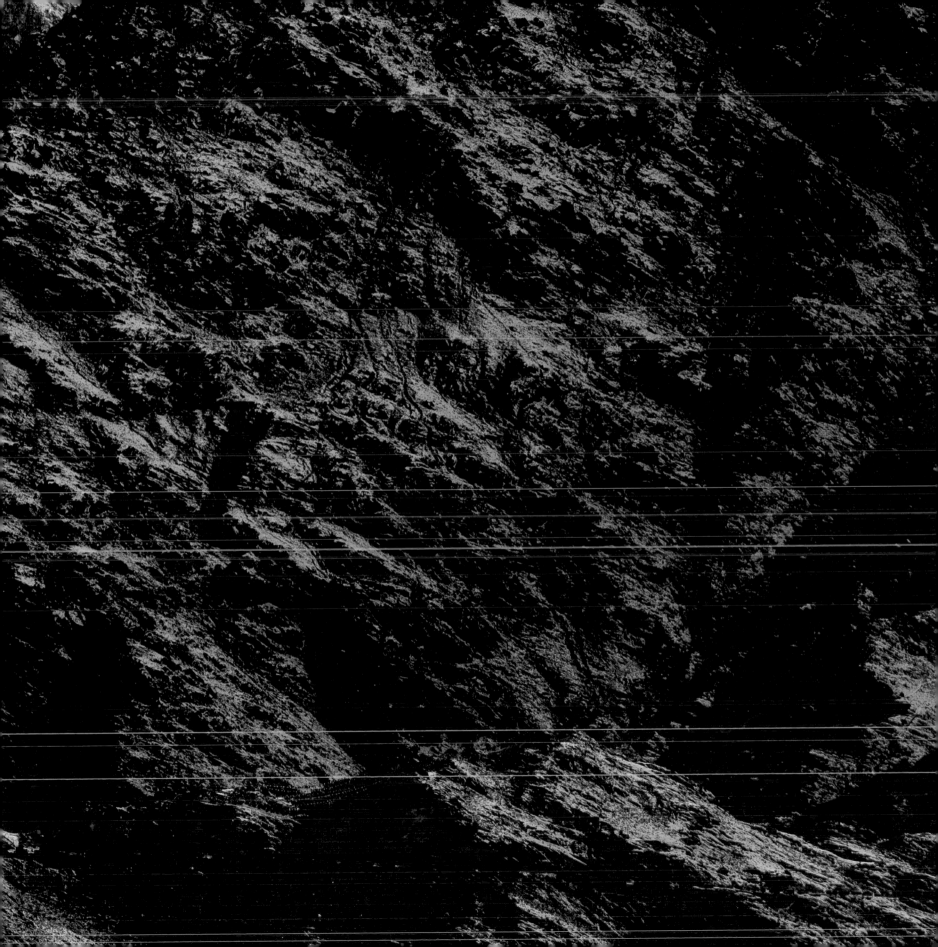

It's sometimes hard to capture the beauty I

see with a camera, but this place was perfect.

The sun came out from behind a cloud to light up

the gorgeous emerald-green hills and cast deep,

long shadows. You have just one chance to capture

the scene. This image is how I picture Ireland

in my dreams.

~George Karbus

COUNTY GALWAY, IRELAND | Stone walls cross an Irish countryside. | *George Karbus*

COUNTY GALWAY, IRELAND | A bridge connects the frosty banks
of a stream. | *Tetra Images*

JOHN DAY FOSSIL BEDS NATIONAL MONUMENT, OREGON | Melting snow reveals the tawny hues of Oregon's Painted Hills. | *Marc Adamus*

SIBERIA, RUSSIA | A horse and rider traverse Lake Baikal's frozen surface. | *Matthieu Paley*

ALBERTA, CANADA | Ice and light paint Jasper National Park. | *Chip Phillips*

NAMIB-NAUKLUFT PARK, NAMIBIA | Sand dunes greet
the Atlantic Ocean. | *Frans Lanting*

DEVON, ENGLAND | A peach tree in the mist | *Adam Burton*

THE KIMBERLEY, WESTERN AUSTRALIA | Water flow and sediment shape
the Ord River Delta. | *Art Wolfe*

"I wanted to photograph the hockey tournament from my motorized paraglider, but freezing temperatures meant I had to hire a helicopter. Even so, sticking your head and hands out the door of a helicopter in 10°F is a numbing experience. It felt appropriate that the little hockey ponds in the picture came out looking like cubes in an outdoor ice tray.

~George Steinmetz

EAGLE RIVER, WISCONSIN | Skaters compete on a patchwork of hockey rinks. | *George Steinmetz*

OPPOSITE: **RIO DE JANEIRO, BRAZIL** | City lights sparkle along Guanabara Bay. | *Mike Theiss*

NEXT PAGES: **KAMCHATKA PENINSULA, RUSSIA** | A high-elevation lake | *Sarah Leen*

Momatiuk - Eastcott/Corbis; 268-9, Carsten Peter/National Geographic Creative; 270-71, © Zoltan Duray/500px Prime; 273, Andrés Miguel Domínguez; 274-5, Chip Phillips; 276-7, Carsten Peter/National Geographic Creative; 278, Michael Melford/National Geographic Creative; 279, Michael Melford/National Geographic Creative; 280-81, Eduard Gutescu/National Geographic Your Shot; 282-3, Michael Melford/National Geographic Creative; 284, Eric Lafforgue/arabianEye/Corbis; 286-7, Diane Cook and Len Jenshel, National Geographic Creative; 288, George Steinmetz/National Geographic Creative; 289, Orsolya Haarberg/National Geographic Creative; 290-91, Matej Kováč /National Geographic Your Shot; 292-3, Kyle Hammons/TandemStock.com; 295, Chip Phillips; 296-7, David Santiago Garcia/Image Broker/Aurora Photos; 298, Adam Burton; 299, Pablo Castagnola/Anzenberger/Redux Pictures; 300-301, Stephen Emerson/Alamy; 302-303, Jim Richardson/National Geographic Creative; 306, Robert Fulton; 308-309, Ido Meirovich/National Geographic Your Shot; 310-11, Christoph Jorda; 312-13, Jim Richardson/National Geographic Creative; 314, Michael Yamashita; 315, Matthew Kuhns/TandemStock.com; 316, Paul Reiffer/National Geographic Your Shot; 318-19, Russell Burden/Getty Images; 320-21, Kyle Hammons/TandemStock.com; 322-3, Chip Phillips; 324-5, Harald Nachtmann/Westend61/Offset; 327, Jassen T/National Geographic Your Shot; 328-9, Dean Conger/National Geographic Creative; 330, Ian Shive/TandemStock.com; 331, Miles Morgan/TandemStock.com; 332-3, Norbert Rosing/National Geographic Creative; 334-5, Chip Phillips; 336-7, Ralph Lee Hopkins/National Geographic Creative; 338, Fabrice Guerin/National Geographic Your Shot; 339, manickam Bala/National Geographic Your Shot; 340-41, Stephen Alvarez/National Geographic Creative; 342-3, Sandra Bartocha/www.bartocha-photography.com; 344, Khalid Al Hammadi/National Geographic Your Shot; 346-7, Adam Burton; 348-9, Tim Laman/National Geographic Creative; 350-51, Andy Clark/Corbis; 352, Hemis/Alamy; 353, Federica Violin/Alamy; 354-5, Paul Marcellini/TandemStock.com; 356-7, Norbert Rosing/National Geographic Creative; 358-9, Jean-Daniel Sudres/Hemis/Corbis; 360-61, Anadolu Agency/Getty Images; 362-3, Daniel Schoenen/Image Broker/Aurora Photos; 365, Mark Lissick; 366-7, Thierry Bornier/National Geographic Your Shot; 368, Pete McBride/National Geographic Creative; 369, Frans Lanting/lanting.com; 370-71, Thierry Bornier/National Geographic Your Shot; 372-3, Erlend Haarberg/Nature Picture Library; 374-5, Art Wolfe/artwolfe.com; 376, George Karbus Photography/Cultura/Aurora Photos; 378-9, Tetra Images/Offset; 380, Marc Adamus; 381, Matthieu Paley; 382-3, Travis Dove/National Geographic Creative; 384-5, Eric DaBreo/National Geographic Your Shot; 386-7, Chip Phillips; 388-9, Frans Lanting/lanting.com; 390, Adam Burton; 391, Art Wolfe/artwolfe.com; 392, George Steinmetz/Corbis; 394-5, Mike Thiess/National Geographic Creative; 396-7, Sarah Leen/National Geographic Creative. ◆

Acknowledgments

Greatest Landscapes was made with the hard work of the National Geographic team and, most important, the talented photographers in the field whose pictures inspire us all.

Special thanks to deputy editor Hilary Black, art director Melissa Farris, photo editor Laura Lakeway, researcher and caption writer Michelle Rae Harris, project editor Anne Smyth, author Susan Hitchcock, photo assistant Patrick Bagley, design production assistant Nicole Miller, as well as countless others who dedicated their time to this book.

Since 1888, the National Geographic Society has funded more than 12,000 research, exploration, and preservation projects around the world. National Geographic Partners distributes a portion of the funds it receives from your purchase to National Geographic Society to support programs including the conservation of animals and their habitats.

National Geographic Partners
1145 17th Street NW
Washington, DC 20036-4688 USA

Become a member of National Geographic and activate your benefits today at natgeo.com/jointoday.

For information about special discounts for bulk purchases, please contact National Geographic Books Special Sales: specialsales@natgeo.com

For rights or permissions inquiries, please contact National Geographic Books Subsidiary Rights: bookrights@natgeo.com

ISBN: 978-1-4262-1712-8

Interior design: Melissa Farris

Printed in China

16/PPS/1

Explore the World with Great Photography Books from National Geographic

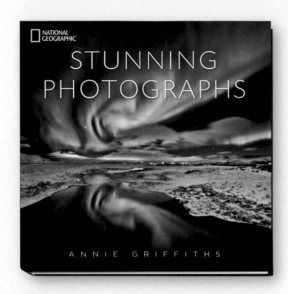

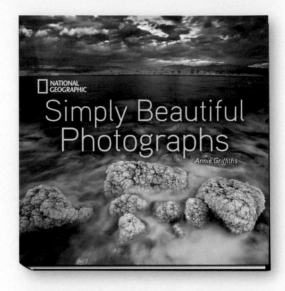

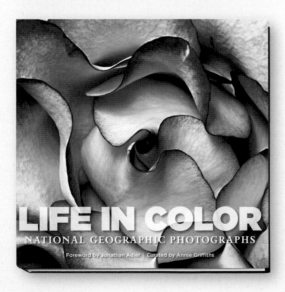

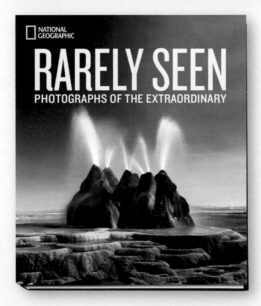